To Maryliz,
Serenità, gioia e speranza,
Lorraine Haddock 2015

Love, peace & joy,
Schuyler

Bella Figlia della Mamma

Mamma's Beautiful Daughter

A bilingual story of mother-daughter love,
the Italian way

LORRAINE HADDOCK

illustrations by
Schuyler McClain & Emily McClain

Copyright © 2015
by Lorraine Haddock.
All rights reserved.

This is a memoir and the names used throughout the book refer only to members of the author's immediate family and do not refer to any other individuals with the same names.

No part of this book may be reproduced or transmitted in any form or by any means, electronic or mechanical, including photocopying, recording, taping or by any information storage retrieval system without the written permission of the copyright owner.

Library of Congress Control Number: 2015949920

ISBN: Hardcover   978-0-692-51572-3

Printed and bound by Edwards Brothers Malloy Inc.
Ann Arbor, Michigan USA

Design by Pinafore Press / Janice Shay
Photography by Kristin McMillan

To order additional copies of this book:
www.brightideastogo.com

To Alexis

A special story for my first grandchild Alexis Lorraine,
celebrating the joy, promise and hope of a new generation.
May you continue the poetry wrapped in the love
of all the women in our family.
"Bella figlia della mamma!"
Love and blessings, Nonna

—L.H.

To Margot Dawson

—S.M. & E.M.

This is a story of six generations of Italian women
beginning from Ascoli Piceno, Italy,
a beautiful medieval city in the Appennini Mountains,
near the Adriatic Sea.

*Questa è la storia di sei generazioni di donne italiane
che ha inizio ad Ascoli Piceno, Italia,
una bella città medievale ai piedi dell'Appennino,
vicino al Mar Adriatico.*

Maria Cicchi

Giulia Gabrielli

Elena Rita

Lorraine Marie

Julia Marie

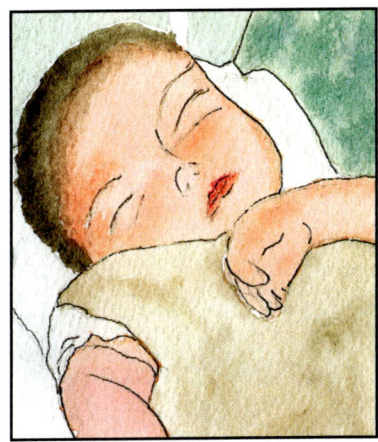

Alexis Lorraine

Maria Cicchi

I am Maria of Ascoli Piceno.

Tomorrow my daughter Giulia departs from Italy,
taking with her the precious linens she has made.
The fabric is common, but elegantly embroidered
in delicate designs, beautifully sewn by her hands.

Gently I touch her initials G G.

Sono Maria, vengo da Ascoli Piceno.

*Domani mia figlia Giulia lascia l'Italia
porta con sé il bel corredo fatto da lei.
Il tessuto è comune, ma elegantemente ricamato
con delicati disegni finemente realizzato con
le sue stesse mani.*

Tocco gentilmente le iniziali G G.

Giulia sits on the bed imagining her future.
Together we fold the linens, carefully
packing them into her luggage.

*Giulia è seduta sul letto e immagina il suo futuro.
Insieme pieghiamo la biancheria con cura
le poniamo nelle valigie.*

For the last time Giulia will walk to the well,
to bring fresh water to our home. I wrap a
linen cloth into a ring and place it on her head.
Together we lift the copper conca
and she stands straight to balance it.

Per l'ultima volta Giulia va al pozzo
per portare acqua fresca a casa.
Io ricavo un anello da un panno di lino
e glielo metto in testa. Insieme alziamo la conca di rame
e lei rimane diritta per tenerla in equilibrio.

I watch my daughter as she walks down the path toward the well.
She is very young and very beautiful.
Tearfully I whisper, "Bella figlia della mamma."

*Guardo mia figlia, mentre cammina verso il pozzo.
Lei è giovanissima e molto bella.
Commossa sussurro "Bella figlia della mamma".*

Giulia Gabrielli

I am Giulia Gabrielli, daughter of Maria.
It is autumn 1920. I wait with my husband
Luigi Fabiani to board the Duke of Abruzzi.
We are going to America. It is a long way.

Sono Giulia Gabrielli, figlia di Maria
È l'autunno del 1920. Attendo con mio marito
Luigi Fabiani di salire a bordo del Duca degli Abruzzi.
Stiamo andando in America. È un lungo viaggio.

Our children are born in the United States. I wrap them in the linens I made when I was a young girl in Italy, and tell them stories of Ascoli Piceno. When our baby daughter is born we call her Elena Rita. It is winter 1927.

I nostri figli sono nati negli Stati Uniti.
Li avvolgo in quelle lenzuola che avevo ricamato
quando ero una giovane ragazza in Italia
e racconto loro le storie di Ascoli Piceno.
Quando nasce la nostra bambina la chiameremo
Elena Rita. È l'inverno del 1927.

My mamma Maria visits from Italy, bringing olive leaves pressed in her prayer book. There are no olive trees in America. She holds Elena close and whispers, "Bella figlia della mamma."

*Mia mamma Maria viene dall'Italia
mi porta foglie di ulivo secche
custodite nel suo libro di preghiera.
Non ci sono alberi di ulivo in America.
Abbraccia forte Elena e sussurra
"Bella figlia della mamma".*

Elena Rita

I am Elena, daughter of Giulia.
When I start elementary school,
I can speak only Italian. As I graduate
from high school I win the English award.
My family is very proud.

*Sono Elena, figlia di Giulia.
Quando inizio la scuola elementare
conosco solo l'italiano. Alle superiori
vinceró un premio per l'inglese.
La mia famiglia è molto orgogliosa di me.*

I marry an American boy.
We call our daughter Lorraine Marie.
It is winter 1950. I wrap her in the linens
my mamma Giulia made when she was
a young girl in Italy, and tell her stories
of Ascoli Piceno.

Mi sposo un ragazzo Americano.
Chiameremo nostra figlia Lorraine Marie.
È l'inverno del 1950. L'avvolgo nelle lenzuola
ricamate da mamma Giulia
quando era giovinetta in Italia
e le racconto le storie di Ascoli Piceno.

My mamma Giulia comes to visit.
She holds Lorraine close and whispers,
"Bella figlia della mamma."

*Mamma Giulia viene a trovarci.
Tiene Lorraine tra le braccia e sussurra
"Bella figlia della mamma".*

Lorraine Marie

I am Lorraine, daughter of Elena.
I visit my nonna Giulia.
She tells me stories of Ascoli Piceno.
Folding a worn linen towel and placing it on her head,
she demonstrates the way she carried water from the well each day,
for her mamma Maria.

Sono Lorraine, figlia di Elena.
Vado a trovare nonna Giulia. Lei mi racconta storie
di Ascoli Piceno. Piegando un logoro asciugamano di lino,
se lo posa sulla testa, mostrandomi come portava
la conca d'acqua ogni giorno dal pozzo,
per la sua mamma Maria.

Nonna Giulia speaks only in Italian.
As we walk together in her garden,
she clips a rose.
I carry it home to my mamma Elena.
Mamma loves roses.

Lei parla solo italiano.
Camminiamo insieme nel suo giardino,
raccoglie una rosa.
Io la porto a casa per mia mamma Elena.
La mamma ama le rose.

When I marry, we call our daughter Julia Marie.
It is summer 1971. I wrap her in the linens my
nonna Giulia made when she was a young girl,
and tell her stories of Ascoli Piceno.

*Quand'io mi sposeró chiameremo nostra figlia Julia Marie.
È l'estate del 1971. L' avvolgo nelle lenzuola ricamate
dalla nonna quand' era giovinetta
e le racconto le storie di Ascoli Piceno.*

Nonna Giulia holds the precious child.
I hear her whisper,
"Bella figlia della mamma."

🌱 🌱 🌱

Nonna Giulia tiene in braccio la dolce bambina.
La sento sussurrare
"Bella figlia della mamma".

Julia Marie

I am Julia, daughter of Lorraine.
My great-grandmom Giulia visits me
when she walks from Mass each morning.
She washes my tiny baby dresses, and brings
biscotti and Italian peach cookies she has made.

Sono Julia, figlia di Lorraine.
La mia bisnonna Giulia viene a trovarmi
quando torna dalla messa ogni mattina.
Lava i miei vestitini e porta i biscotti
e i dolcetti italiani alla pesca che lei ha fatto.

My mamma Lorraine prepares the crema and the pasta
and the stuffed olives of the Marches region.
Speaking with enthusiasm and pride,
she tells the Italian history of our family.
She speaks a little Italian with my nonna Elena
and writes letters to our cousins in Ascoli Piceno.

*Mamma Lorraine prepara la crema, e la pasta
e le olive all'ascolana delle Marche.
Racconta le storie della nostra famiglia
parlandone con entusiasmo e orgoglio.
Parla un po' in italiano con nonna Elena
e scrive lettere ai cugini di Ascoli Piceno.*

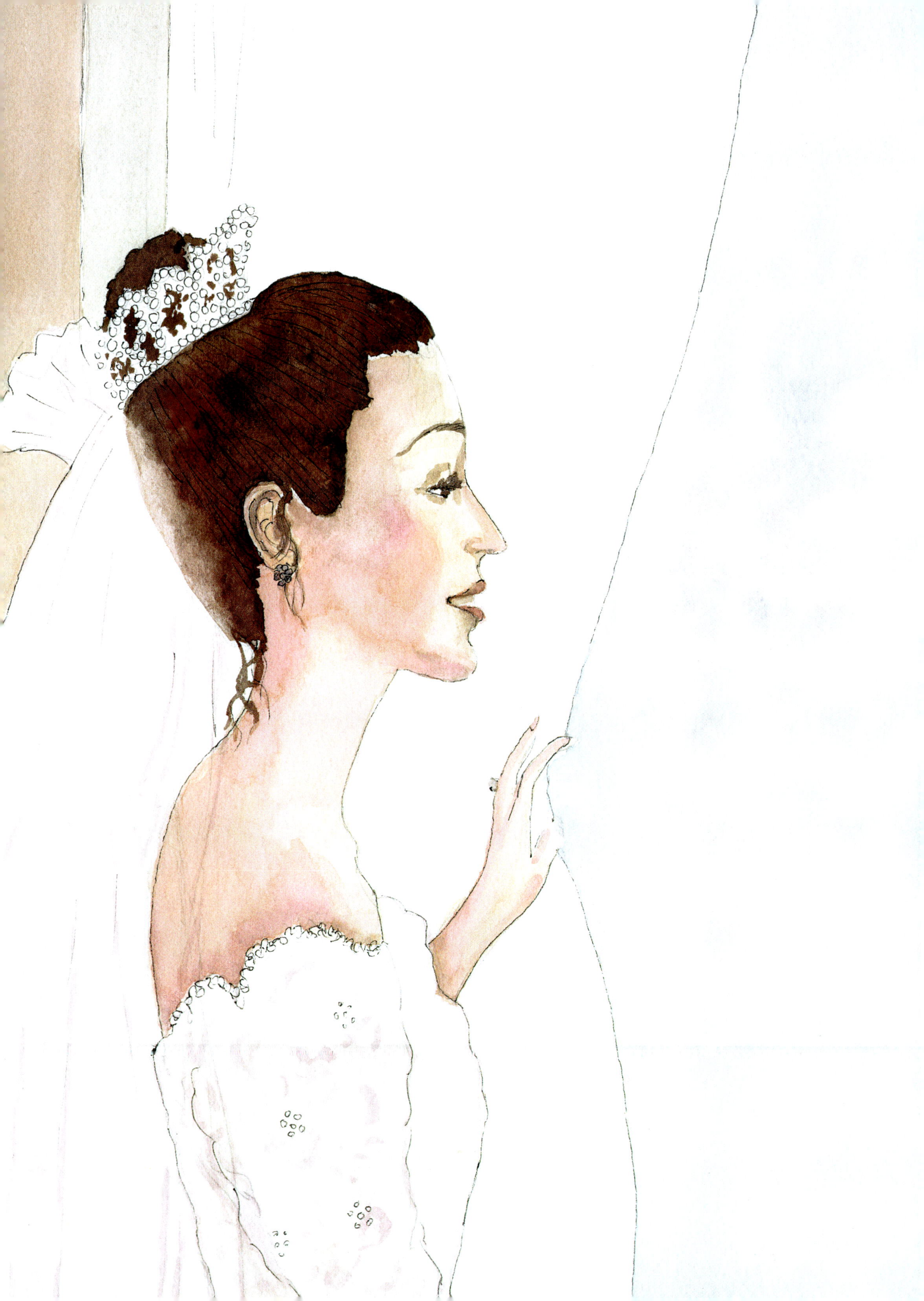

I marry, and my mamma Lorraine folds the precious linens
that Giulia made, when she was a young girl in Italy.
I take the delicate linens to my new home
and gently touch the initials G G.

*Io mi sposo e mamma Lorraine piega le lenzuola
che aveva fatto Giulia quand'era giovinetta in Italia.
Porto la biancheria delicata nella mia nuova casa.
Con dolcezza tocco le iniziali G G.*

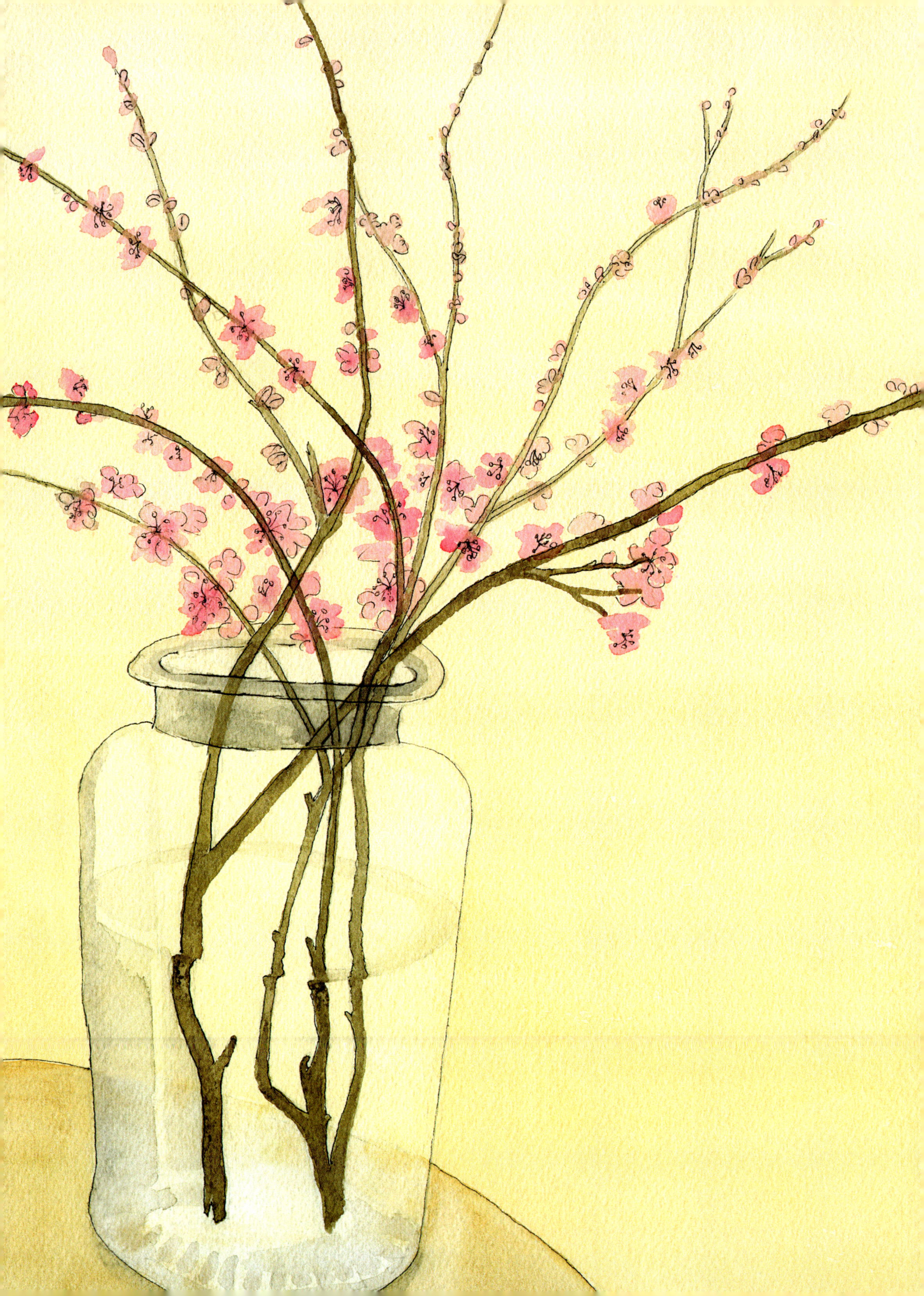

We call our daughter Alexis Lorraine.
It is springtime 2000.
My mamma Lorraine visits,
bringing peach blossoms.

*Chiameremo nostra figlia Alexis Lorraine.
È la primavera del 2000.
Mamma Lorraine viene a trovarci
e ci porta un ramoscello di fior di pesco.*

She holds Alexis very close.
I hear her whisper,
"Bella figlia della mamma."

*Stringe forte Alexis.
La sento sussurrare
"Bella figlia della mamma".*

Alexis Lorraine

I am Alexis daughter of Julia.
My story is just beginning… .

Sono Alexis, figlia di Julia.
La mia storia è solo all'inizio… .

Glossary

ITALIAN	ENGLISH
FAMIGLIA	FAMILY
bambina	baby girl
bisnonna	great-grandmother
cugini	cousins
figlia	daughter
mamma	mother (mom)
marito	husband
nonna	grandmother

CIBI TRADIZIONALE   TRADITIONAL FOODS

biscotti – biscuit-type Italian cookies flavored with anise.

crema – a sweet pudding served over pound cake and garnished with cinnamon sticks and spirals of lemon peel.

dolcetti italiani alla pesca – Italian cream-filled cookies shaped to look like a peach.

olive all'ascolana – large green olives stuffed with a meat filling. and fried in olive oil   A famous food of Ascoli Piceno.

pasta – home-made spaghetti, gnocchi and ravioli.

Glossary

ITALIAN	ENGLISH
STAGIONI	SEASONS
autunno	autumn
estate	summer
inverno	winter
primavera	spring
ALTRE PAROLE ED ESPRESSIONI	OTHER WORDS AND EXPRESSIONS

biancheria / lenzuola – linens, towels, pillowcases and bedding for the home, often woven from flax yarns and embellished with embroidery.

la conca di rame – a large copper vessel designed to carry water.

corredo – trousseau, a bride's linens she brings with her when she marries.

libro di preghiera – book of prayers.

le Marche – the Marches, a region of central Italy in the Appennini Mountains along the Adriatic Sea.

molto bella – very beautiful.

Artists
Schuyler McClain

Schuyler McClain was born and raised on Absecon Island off the coast of New Jersey. She grew up in Margate in a home adorned with her mother's numerous and masterful paintings. Schuyler drew inspiration for much of her artwork while walking the beaches of the Jersey shore.

Schuyler received her Bachelor of Arts in Art Education and a Master of Arts in Environmental Education from Glassboro College (now Rowan University). She taught elementary school art for 30 years in New Jersey public schools and was a teacher of art at The University of the Arts Saturday School in Philadelphia. Currently retired from education, she is a working artist residing in Moorestown, NJ, with her husband Geoffrey and their daughter Emily.

Schuyler is a member of the Perkins Center for the Arts and the Burlington County Art Guild, showing her work in juried art shows. In 2014 she illustrated *Giving Thanks*, a cookbook for the First Presbyterian Church in Moorestown, NJ. Schuyler's chosen media include pen and ink, colored pencil and watercolor.

Emily McClain

Emily McClain has been surrounded by art from the day she was born. Her grandmother, Margot Dawson, who lived to the age of 100, was a full-time artist whose home was covered in paintings from the floor to the ceiling. Her mother, an elementary art teacher, was constantly creating new pieces of artwork in the studio. Her father has always had an interest in photography and now shows his work in galleries.

It is no surprise that Emily enjoys creating artwork herself. To design her work, she uses pencil, acrylic paint on canvas and watercolor. Pencil allows her to be detailed and sketch out ideas, while acrylic and watercolor let her play with vivid color and brush strokes.

Throughout her life, art has been the one thing that truly sets her apart from her peers, making her feel successful and important and bringing her joy and confidence. Emily states, "My art defines me, and I couldn't imagine living life without it." She has studied art at the Moore College of Art & Design and the University of the Arts in Philadelphia. Emily attends The College of New Jersey.

Author
Lorraine Haddock, of the family Fabiani

American-born author Lorraine Haddock received her Bachelor of Arts degree in English from Rowan University. In *Bella Figlia della Mamma*, her first bilingual book, she shares her family memories. This heartwarming story was originally written as a poem to celebrate the birth of her granddaughter Alexis.

Lorraine loves sharing her experiences through poetry and storytelling. Her real-life stories spring from childhood memories, close relationships with the remarkable women who have shaped her life and the joy of being a mother. Very proud of her Italian heritage, she hopes to promote the language and culture of Italy by sharing this story with readers of all ages.

The author is currently working on a series of children's books titled, *Nonna! Nonna! Tell us a Story!* Her first book, *The Duck Without A Quack*, a true story of her lovable pet duckling, was released in February 2015.

In addition to writing, Lorraine is a skilled fiber artist following the tradition of her nonna, Giulia Gabrielli Fabiani. Passionate about creative sewing, Lorraine is a member of The American Sewing Guild and The Third Star Fibre Artists Guild, displaying her work and demonstrating hand embroidery at art shows in southern New Jersey.

Lorraine encourages all parents and grandparents to share their stories and family memories. She hopes *Bella Figlia della Mamma* will be treasured and shared by mothers and daughters everywhere.

Acknowledgments

My grateful thanks to:

Schuyler McClain, for her beautiful artwork rendered in watercolor and for her lifelong friendship.

Emily McClain, for sketching the storyboard and creating several illustrations for the book.

Dr. Maria Elisa Chiavarelli, 1938-2013, professor of romance languages at Rowan University, for helping me to translate an early version of this story while I attended her Italian class at Rowan in 2005.

Roberta Polimanti Cornwall, language teacher and tutor in Teramo, Italy, for revisions and editing and for sharing a love of the Italian language.

Fabio Capolla, journalist and poet in Teramo, Italy, for advice, revisions and editing of the Italian text.

Sr. Maria DiRosa, FMIJ (Franciscan Missionary of the Infant Jesus) St. Clare of Assisi Parish, Gibbstown, NJ, for guidance and encouragement in the language, culture and faith of the Italian people.

Kristin McMillan Photography, Sopchoppy, FL, for professional photographs of the antique linens made by my nonna, Giulia Gabrielli.

Elena Rita, my mother; Julia Marie, my daughter; and Alexis Lorraine, my granddaughter; for taking part in this special story.

My relatives and friends in Ascoli Piceno, Italy, who always welcome my family and me with open arms, giving us a sense of belonging in their ancient and beautiful city, as if we were born there.